Earthquakes and Volcanoes

Earthquakes and Volcanoes

Alison Rae

Smart Apple Media

First published in 2005 by Evans Brothers Limited
2A Portman Mansions, Chiltern Street
London W1U 6NR

Consultant: Simon Ross, Editor: Sonya Newland, Designer: Big Blu Ltd.,
Picture Researcher: Julia Bird

Published in the United States by Smart Apple Media
2140 Howard Drive West, North Mankato, Minnesota 56003

Library of Congress Cataloging-in-Publication Data

Rae, Alison.
Earthquakes and volcanoes / by Alison Rae.
p. cm. — (Looking at landscapes)
Includes bibliographical references and index.
ISBN 1-58340-729-4
1. Earthquakes—Juvenile literature. 2. Volcanoes—Juvenile literature. I. Title. II. Series.

QE521.3.R34 2005
551.2—dc22   2005040501

9 8 7 6 5 4 3 2 1

Contents

Introduction

Earthquakes and volcanoes are among the most spectacular and dangerous natural hazards on the planet—they have been occurring for millions of years and still happen today. This activity largely takes place at the boundaries where Earth's plates meet, either colliding or grinding past one another.

Sometimes the movement of these plates causes red-hot molten rock to bubble up through Earth's crust. Great pressure in the areas beneath Earth's surface forces this magma upward in a great explosion, creating a volcano. When volcanoes erupt, they can eject lava as well as dust and rock. Over time, this hardens and builds up to form layers that become part of a distinctive volcanic landscape. In other regions, the great force caused by the plates meeting makes Earth shake, sometimes resulting in great cracks on Earth's surface and sending out shock waves for many miles.

▼ The magnificent but deadly firework displays caused by volcanoes, such as this one in Iceland, are some of the most impressive features of the natural world.

▲ Earthquakes such as the one that hit Mexico City in 1985 can cause severe damage and loss of life.

Some parts of the world suffer terribly from the effects of plate activity. Whole settlements can be destroyed and often are not rebuilt because of the emotional pain involved. When an earthquake strikes, buildings and other structures collapse, killing many people and devastating entire cities. Sometimes earthquakes even cause tsunamis—massive waves that can sweep onto land, washing away everything in their path. Seismologists record hundreds of earthquakes every year, but only a few of them are severe enough to cause serious damage. When a volcano erupts, even if the lava flow poses no immediate threat, the enormous clouds of dust and ash can spread great distances and cover a region in a thick, suffocating blanket. However, this can create very fertile land, which is useful for cultivation.

Despite the danger these natural hazards pose, many people still live in areas where they take place. In poorer countries, this is often because the inhabitants do not have the means to move to a safer region. In other parts of the world, people believe that the advantages outweigh the risks, and they are willing to stay. As technology progresses and our understanding of earthquakes and volcanoes increases, scientists are better able to predict when they might occur and to prepare for the disaster they may cause. Whatever measures are taken, though, earthquakes and volcanic eruptions will remain a constant reminder of the immense power of natural forces on our planet.

▼ Scientists study these natural phenomena in the hope of predicting when and where an eruption or earthquake is likely to occur. Here, a scientist takes a measurement of lava flow on La Fournaise volcano in the Indian Ocean.

What Causes Earthquakes and Volcanoes?

Ⓘf we could dig through Earth's surface to its center, we would see that it has four layers.

Earth's core—inner and outer together—has a diameter of nearly 2,175 miles (3,500 km) and is larger than our neighboring planet, Mars. The temperature of Earth's core is about 11,200 °F (6,200 °C)—hotter than the surface of the sun. Toward the surface, temperatures decrease, but even the lower parts of the crust can be as hot as 2,200 °F (1,200 °C). Earth's surface is characterized by a series of gigantic plates of different sizes and shapes. Because Earth's plates actually move in relation to each other, a great deal of activity takes place at their boundaries or margins.

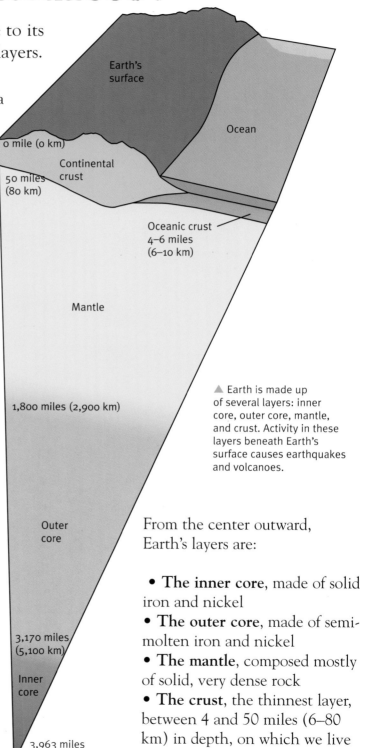

Earth's surface

Ocean

0 mile (0 km)

Continental crust

50 miles (80 km)

Oceanic crust 4–6 miles (6–10 km)

Mantle

1,800 miles (2,900 km)

▲ Earth is made up of several layers: inner core, outer core, mantle, and crust. Activity in these layers beneath Earth's surface causes earthquakes and volcanoes.

Outer core

3,170 miles (5,100 km)

Inner core

3,963 miles (6,378 km)

🔴 Earth's crust

The thickness of Earth's crust relative to the rest of the planet has been described in a number of ways: it is as thin as the skin of an apple compared to the rest of the fruit, or it is like a postage stamp stuck to a soccerball. The crust is of two types—oceanic and continental. Oceanic crust forms the seabed and is made of a dense rock called basalt. Continental crust sits on top of some of the oceanic crust. Up to 50 miles (80 km) thick, it is made up of less dense rocks, such as granite.

From the center outward, Earth's layers are:

• **The inner core**, made of solid iron and nickel
• **The outer core**, made of semi-molten iron and nickel
• **The mantle**, composed mostly of solid, very dense rock
• **The crust**, the thinnest layer, between 4 and 50 miles (6–80 km) in depth, on which we live and about which we know most

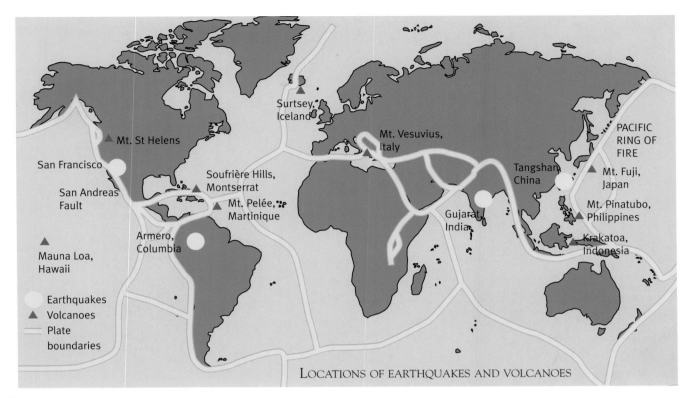

Surtsey, Iceland

Mt. St Helens

San Francisco

San Andreas Fault

Mauna Loa, Hawaii

Soufrière Hills, Montserrat

Mt. Pelée, Martinique

Armero, Columbia

Mt. Vesuvius, Italy

Tangshan China

Gujarat, India

PACIFIC RING OF FIRE

Mt. Fuji, Japan

Mt. Pinatubo, Philippines

Krakatoa, Indonesia

○ Earthquakes
▲ Volcanoes
— Plate boundaries

LOCATIONS OF EARTHQUAKES AND VOLCANOES

Plate tectonics

Plate tectonics is a theory, developed in the 1960s, about Earth's plates—how they were formed, how they move, and the results of their movements. The most dramatic earthquake and volcanic action happens at plate boundaries, but the precise nature of this activity depends on the direction of plate movement.

At constructive margins, plates move away from each other, magma from the mantle rises to fill the space, and the solidified magma forms new crust. These constructive zones can be found beneath the oceans as enormous ridges, such as the Mid-Atlantic Ridge. Volcanoes are common at these margins. Earthquakes do occur, but they tend not to be very destructive.

At destructive boundaries, two plates move toward each other, and crust is destroyed. At subduction zones, one plate is forced downward beneath the overriding plate. As the oceanic plate subducts (moves down) below the continental plate, rising temperatures and friction cause the oceanic rocks to melt and turn into magma. Some of the magma rises to the surface through cracks in the

▲ It is easy to see a relationship between the locations of volcanoes and earthquakes, and the boundaries of Earth's plates. However, there are a few volcanoes that exist far away from the plate margins. These are called intraplate volcanoes, and they are located over hot spots, where plumes of magma (liquid or molten rock) break through relatively thin parts of the crust.

▲ Iceland is the only part of the Mid-Atlantic Ridge that rises above sea level, and its central volcanic plateau is erupting almost constantly.

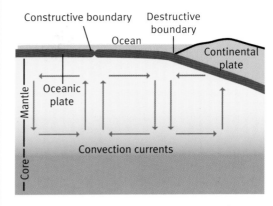

Constructive boundary   Destructive boundary

Ocean

Continental plate

Mantle

Oceanic plate

Core

Convection currents

▲ Plates move because of processes that take place within the mantle. The rocks in the mantle are not always solid. Pressure increases with depth, which in turn leads to an increase in temperature. At certain depths, the rock of the mantle reaches its melting point, and magma is produced. This then rises toward the surface, from high pressure deep down to relatively low pressure nearer the surface. Scientists believe that there are circular currents of heat called convection currents operating within the mantle, which are responsible for the movement of the plates.

▶ At constructive boundaries, two plates move away from each other, and volcanoes often occur.

▶ At destructive boundaries, one plate can override another, forming a subduction zone, where earthquakes can occur as the plates stick to each other, then jolt free.

▶ Another feature of destructive boundaries is an island arc—chains of underwater volcanoes formed by the subducted plate melting and forming magma.

continental plate, forming volcanoes with sometimes explosive activity. As the two plates slide past and over each other, substantial friction stores energy within the rocks. The plates can become stuck, and the jolt experienced on the surface of Earth when they finally pull apart is an earthquake.

Two continental plates moving toward each other cause earthquakes but not volcanoes. This is because the plates are relatively light and tend to crumple rather than subduct. With no subduction, there is no formation of magma to feed volcanoes. The immense crumpling pressures push up huge mountain ranges such as the Alps and the Himalayas. This type of plate margin is called a collision zone.

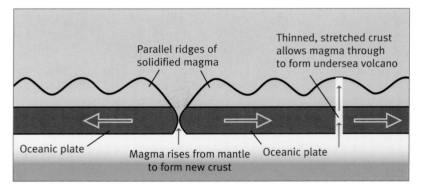

Parallel ridges of solidified magma

Thinned, stretched crust allows magma through to form undersea volcano

Oceanic plate   Magma rises from mantle to form new crust   Oceanic plate

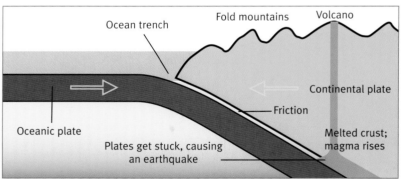

Ocean trench   Fold mountains   Volcano

Continental plate

Friction

Oceanic plate

Plates get stuck, causing an earthquake

Melted crust; magma rises

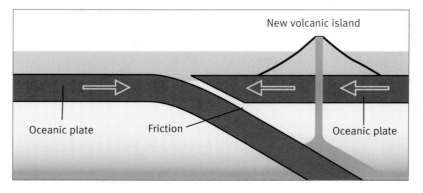

New volcanic island

Oceanic plate   Friction   Oceanic plate

Fault lines

A fault is a crack in the rocks of Earth's crust, where one section of rock has moved relative to the other. Faulting is caused by plate movement and can occur either vertically or horizontally.

Faults that move rocks horizontally form another type of plate margin, known as a conservative boundary. These are different from all others because the two plates move beside each other instead of toward or away from each other. No new crust is formed, and no existing crust is destroyed. There is no volcanic activity, but it is along these fault lines that earthquakes most frequently occur.

▲ The Great Rift Valley in East Africa is a different kind of fault line. Some scientists think it is a new constructive plate margin about to open up. This huge valley is 3,100 miles (5,000 km) long, and in places, it is more than half a mile (1 km) deep. It contains volcanoes such as Mount Kilimanjaro in Tanzania, now thought to be extinct. At 19,340 feet (5,895 m), Kilimanjaro is the highest mountain in Africa.

▶ At a conservative plate margin, friction is generated and energy stored as the rocks along the edges of the plates move past each other. In the same way as at destructive boundaries, sometimes the two sides become stuck, and only a severe jolt can shake them loose. Shock waves called seismic waves spread out in all directions. It is this sudden jolt, or release of pressure, that causes an earthquake.

⬤ The San Andreas Fault

The most famous fault in the world, the San Andreas Fault, causes earthquakes in one of America's richest and most densely populated urban areas. Stretching right through California and southward into Mexico, the fault is 700 miles (1,125 km) long. The San Andreas Fault is unusual, however, because the plates on either side of it, the Pacific and the North American, are not moving in opposite directions. Instead, both are moving approximately northwestward, but they are doing so at different speeds—two inches (6 cm) per year for the Pacific plate, and one-third inch (1 cm) per year for the North American plate.

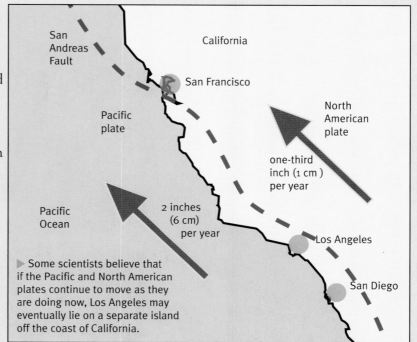

San Andreas Fault

California

San Francisco

North American plate

Pacific plate

one-third inch (1 cm) per year

Pacific Ocean

2 inches (6 cm) per year

Los Angeles

San Diego

▶ Some scientists believe that if the Pacific and North American plates continue to move as they are doing now, Los Angeles may eventually lie on a separate island off the coast of California.

The Quaking Earth

Earthquakes occur at all types of plate margins. They tend to be most powerful where huge pressures build up, such as at destructive and conservative plate margins and at collision zones. With the exception of Antarctica, all continents experience earthquakes. When an earthquake occurs, a shock or jolt takes place at a point underground known as the focus. The energy spreads out from the focus as a series of seismic, or shock, waves. These are most powerful immediately around the focus and become weaker with distance. The point on Earth's surface vertically above the focus is the epicenter. People living here usually feel the maximum force of the earthquake's energy.

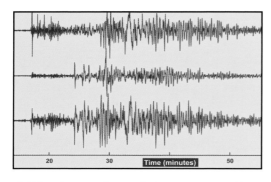

▲ This seismograph records the waves caused by the earthquake that hit Afghanistan in March 2002. These readings were taken thousands of miles away in Edinburgh, Scotland. The seismic waves took about 15 minutes to travel through Earth from Afghanistan to Scotland.

▶ The two main types of earthquake waves are P waves and S waves. S waves move from side to side. P waves move forward through Earth like a coiled spring.

Seismic waves

Three different types of earthquake waves exist: P waves (primary or "push" waves); S waves (secondary or "shake" waves); and L waves (longitudinal or "surface" waves). Both P and S waves start at the focus, but they move in different ways. P waves move like a "slinky" toy; energy pulses forward from the focus. S waves behave more like a rope being waved from one end, shaking the ground back and forth. L waves are very complex waves that move close to the surface. They have high amplitudes and can be very destructive to property.

P wave

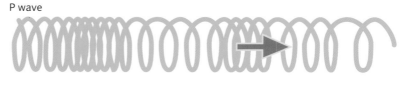

S wave

Each type of wave travels at a different speed. P waves are the fastest and L the slowest. On a seismogram (a graph showing the pattern of earthquake waves), the P waves are drawn first, because they move more quickly. Scientists can figure out how far away the focus of an earthquake is by recording the time difference between when P and S waves reach a particular point away from the earthquake. P waves travel through both solids and liquids, but S waves do not pass through liquids. This means they bounce off Earth's liquid inner core. From careful measurement of this behavior, scientists have figured out the size and composition of the layers of our planet.

In a few earthquakes, seismic waves have behaved unusually because of the physical geography of the area. Mexico City suffered severely when an earthquake hit in 1985, yet it was far from the epicenter and should have been fairly safe. The city is built on an old lake bed made of soft sediments. The seismic waves made the ground wobble like jelly, causing many buildings to collapse or simply sink into the soft ground. Only a small part of the city is built on solid rock. Today, this area is much in demand and has the highest housing prices.

▲ The Mexico City earthquake in 1985 caused hundreds of buildings to collapse, killing or injuring thousands of people.

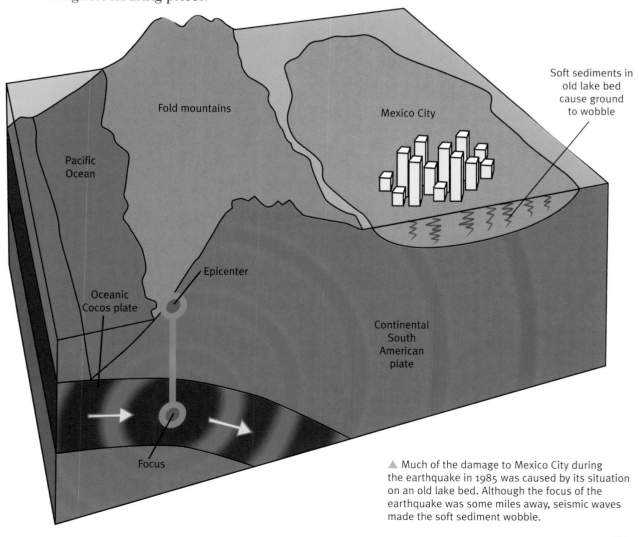

Soft sediments in old lake bed cause ground to wobble

Fold mountains

Mexico City

Pacific Ocean

Epicenter

Oceanic Cocos plate

Continental South American plate

Focus

▲ Much of the damage to Mexico City during the earthquake in 1985 was caused by its situation on an old lake bed. Although the focus of the earthquake was some miles away, seismic waves made the soft sediment wobble.

In December 2003, an earthquake measuring 6.6 on the Richter scale hit the city of Bam in Iran. It also measured high on the Mercalli scale—70 percent of the city was destroyed.

Charles Richter, who devised the scale that is named after him, pictured here with his seismograph.

Measuring earthquakes

The Richter scale is the most common scale for measuring the magnitude of earthquakes. It is a logarithmic scale, which means that each point is 10 times greater than the one below it. Thus, a magnitude 7 earthquake is 10 times larger than one of magnitude 6, 100 times larger than magnitude 5, and 1,000 times larger than magnitude 4. This is an open-ended scale, since it is based on measurements instead of descriptions. Major world earthquakes usually measure 6.0 or higher on the Richter scale.

The Mercalli scale examines the effects of the event, including how much damage is done. This scale does not need instruments to measure it; it can all be done by observation. The Mercalli scale has 12 intensity ratings:

I People do not feel any movement.
II When standing still or on the upper floors of tall buildings, a slight movement might be noticed.
III Hanging objects swing back and forth.

IV Dishes, windows, and doors rattle. Parked cars rock.

V Sleeping people wake up. Doors swing, liquids spill, trees shake.

VI People have trouble walking. Furniture moves, plaster cracks, and things fall from shelves and hooks. No real structural damage yet.

VII People have difficulty standing. Moving cars shake. Loose materials fall from buildings.

VIII Drivers have trouble steering. Towers and chimneys might fall. Poorly built buildings suffer severe damage, but well-constructed ones are only slightly damaged.

IX Well-constructed buildings suffer considerable damage. Underground pipes break. The ground cracks.

X Most buildings are destroyed. Dams are broken, and landslides occur. Roads and railways crack or bend.

XI Most buildings and bridges collapse. Large cracks appear in the ground.

XII Almost everything is destroyed. Ground moves in waves.

▲ Seismologists use a variety of recording and timing equipment to measure seismic waves and to gauge a picture of the rock strata below Earth's surface in earthquake-prone areas. Artificial seismic wave generators send shock waves into Earth, and any breaks in the rock strata are recorded on machines like the ones pictured. This can help warn of an impending earthquake.

◀ This aerial photograph shows the damage caused by an earthquake in California in 1994. This part of Los Angeles was over the epicenter of the earthquake, which measured 6.6 on the Richter scale. At the top center, a department store and parking ramp have collapsed. A train has also been derailed, blocking a road (bottom right).

Effects in different countries

The San Andreas Fault, dividing the North American and Pacific plates, is one of the best-known earthquake zones in the world. Activity here affects a More Economically Developed Country (MEDC). Severe earthquakes hit San Francisco in both 1906 and 1989, and Los Angeles in 1994.

The northeast Indian state of Gujarat is close to a collision zone, where the Indo-Australian plate meets the Eurasian plate. As a Less Economically Developed Country (LEDC), this region of India suffered severely in the 2001 earthquake.

MEDCs have the money and technology to protect themselves from many of the effects of earthquakes. LEDCs, however, are in a much worse position. Most people can only afford basic homes, made from cheap materials; these can collapse easily, killing those inside.

MEDCs can afford better-equipped, well-trained emergency services. Help reaches people more quickly. In LEDCs, communication is often so poor that help is slow in coming. Earthquakes usually occur without warning. In MEDCs, people almost always know whether or not they live in a high-risk zone. They are educated in what to do to in the event of an earthquake. In LEDCs, communication is worse, and people are less aware of protection measures.

▼ Although earthquakes—like this one that derailed a train (pictured) in Los Angeles in 1994—can cause havoc in MEDCs, the damage and loss of life is often far less than in LEDCs because emergency services are well-trained and communication more efficient.

The San Francisco earthquakes

The great earthquake of 1906 began at 5:12 A.M. on April 18; the ground shook for 45 to 60 seconds. Measuring 8.25 on the Richter scale, it remains the largest quake recorded along the San Andreas Fault. Approximately 700 deaths were reported, but many believe the true figure was 3 or 4 times higher.

People were injured or killed by collapsing buildings and by fires that broke out over the city from fractured gas pipes. Older, wooden buildings proved more resistant to the shaking, but were at greater risk from the fires. In fact, fires caused far more destruction than the ground shaking.

▲ During the 1906 San Francisco earthquake, fires broke out across the city and burned for three days. Most of the city center was destroyed as the fires spread.

The 1989 quake caused fewer deaths. Most were on the double-decker Cypress freeway in Oakland. Although the city was better prepared for the 1989 earthquake, due to technological improvements, the cost of the damage was still more than $6 billion. It was America's most expensive natural disaster to date.

Warning signs

Scientific earthquake prediction is not always accurate, but sometimes there are warning signs before an earthquake strikes. Large earthquakes release enormous amounts of energy in the form of seismic waves. Some of the energy that builds up in Earth's crust "leaks out" prior to the catastrophic event. The buildup of high electric fields where the rock meets the air may provide an explanation for reported occurrences of pre-earthquake "ground-

● The Bhuj earthquake

The city of Bhuj in India was almost at the epicenter of a 7.9 magnitude earthquake, which occurred on January 26, 2001. The 45-second shake caused a huge amount of damage. Places far from the epicenter were also devastated because their buildings collapsed so easily. In Ahmedabad, 275 miles (443 km) from Bhuj, where the population is around 5 million, more than 100 buildings were destroyed. Many structures were made of heavy, reinforced concrete, which is easily

▲ When the massive earthquake struck Bhuj in the Indian province of Gujarat in 2001, the city and surrounding villages suffered severely. The loss of life was more than it might have been because it was a national holiday; more people than usual were at home and were buried as their houses collapsed. These men look at a car buried under the wreckage of a collapsed building.

wrecked by shaking. Roofs were flat and made of a single section, so when they collapsed, people trapped underneath were literally buried alive. Those who survived had lost everything.

An earthquake measuring 7.8 on the Richter scale hit Tangshan in China on July 28, 1976. Most people lost their livelihoods (78 percent of industries were destroyed), and the vast majority were left homeless (93 percent of houses were destroyed).

hugging fog." Electrically charged particles in the air might explain why animals seem to behave in a strange, agitated way before an earthquake; the particles could also be the cause of the luminous phenomena known as "earthquake lights." Unusual lights and sounds were reported the night before the Tangshan earthquake in 1976.

Tsunamis

Tsunamis are huge ocean waves caused by an earthquake or volcanic eruption beneath the sea. If they hit land they can cause severe damage. The extent of this depends on how far the wave has travelled before it hits land. The longer the distance, the less energy the wave has remaining; but the further the wave travels the greater its height. The shape of the coastline is also significant. Coastlines that slope gently into the sea and bays that narrow quickly inland both concentrate energy and make the waves higher and stronger, and the potential damage worse. The intensity of a tsunami is gauged by its wave height:

Tsunamis can be caused by earthquakes or volcanic eruptions. This painting depicts the wave caused by the eruption of Krakatoa in 1883.

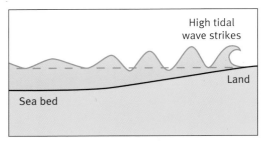

High tidal wave strikes

Land

Sea bed

▲ A gently sloping coast allows a tsunami to grow higher.

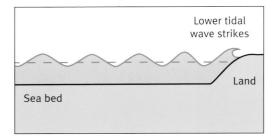

Lower tidal wave strikes

Land

Sea bed

▲ Along a steeper coast, the wave is not able to build as much as on a gentle slope.

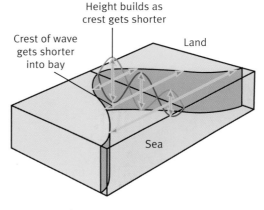

Height builds as crest gets shorter

Crest of wave gets shorter into bay

Land

Sea

▲ The longer the crest, the more energy there is in the wave—a bay shortens the length of the crest, concentrating the energy, which makes the tsunami higher.

▶ Aceh in northern Indonesia was the first inhabited area hit by the Asian tsunami in December 2004. Here, a man walks through the wreckage caused by the giant waves.

1.5 feet (.5 m): very slight; not noticed; occurs often.

3 feet (1 m): slight to medium; low-lying coasts are flooded; occurs approximately once every four to eight months.

13 feet (4 m): flooding; some damage to coastal buildings; lots of debris and litter; occurs approximately once a year.

26 feet (8 m): very large; small buildings destroyed, large ones damaged; drownings; fish and sea mammals washed ashore; occurs approximately once every three years.

52 feet (16 m): disastrous; almost all buildings totally destroyed; trees uprooted; ships badly damaged; many deaths and injuries; occurs approximately once every 10 years.

The Asian tsunami of December 2004 fell into the last category. With waves reaching 40 feet (15 m) in height as they hit land, this was one of the worst natural disasters in living memory—more than 220,000 people were killed almost instantly, and it is estimated that a further 150,000 will die from disease in the wake of the disaster. Witnesses said they heard a sound like the roaring of a jet plane before the waves struck, and whole communities were wiped out in a matter of seconds.

One reason for the extent of the damage is that no warning system exists in the Indian Ocean, where the undersea earthquake that caused the tsunami occurred. Ninety percent of the world's most powerful tsunamis happen in the Pacific Ocean. This area is called the Pacific Ring of Fire (see page 29) because so many volcanoes and earthquakes happen here. There are plate margins all around the Pacific. Four hundred tsunamis occur here every year, although most are small. Japan and Taiwan are affected by about a quarter of these. Pacific tsunamis can travel at 500 miles (800 km) per hour and cross the whole ocean in less than a day.

Systems warning of an approaching tsunami have been operating in some parts of the Pacific Ocean since 1948. This Pacific Warning System is based in Honolulu, Hawaii, and helps to warn 24 countries of approaching danger. Its 100 seismic and tidal stations are spread across the ocean. They try to give any area at risk at least one hour to prepare and evacuate. By the time scientists working here had registered the Asian tsunami, it was too late to begin proper evacuation procedures in the countries at risk.

Tsunami damage

There are three main ways in which tsunamis cause damage:
• Whole buildings can be picked up and moved inland. Sometimes they are pulled out to sea as the wave goes back (hydrostatic effects).
• Debris carried by the wave can be thrown at buildings and people, causing damage (shock effects).
• The shock of being hit by something so powerful smashes roads, bridges, and harbors (hydrodynamic effects).

▼ This aerial view shows the waters of the tsunami receding from the coastal area of Kalutara in Sri Lanka. As the waters swirled back, they carried wreckage with them.

The Asian tsunami

On December 26, 2004, plate movement deep beneath the Indian Ocean triggered an earthquake off the coast of Sumatra. Measuring 9.0 on the Richter scale, the earthquake created huge amounts of energy that sent shock waves out in all directions. The resulting tsunami sped across the ocean, gaining height as it approached land, and eventually crashed into coastlines across Asia. Even Africa, 3,100 miles (5,000 km) from the epicenter, was affected. Many people were unaware of the danger they were in; some even rushed to the water's edge to see what was happening. People drowned and buildings and vehicles were destroyed as the waves enveloped coastal areas and then sucked the debris back out to sea.

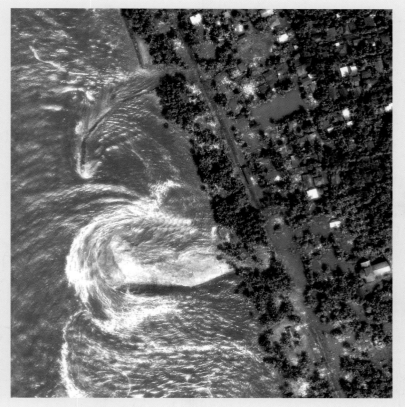

Mountains of Fire

There are several types of volcanoes, and they are all shaped differently because of the various processes responsible for their formation. Despite having very different shapes and characteristics, all volcanoes have some features in common. Their sides may be built of different materials, but they all have a vent—a hole in the middle where the magma rises to the surface. Magma varies in its chemical composition and temperature, and both of these factors affect the size and shape of the volcano. Most volcanoes have a magma chamber, a large space underground where molten rock from the mantle collects. The pressure builds up, and the magma pushes harder to break through Earth's surface, until eventually it does so in a volcanic eruption. Magma that reaches the surface is called lava. Lava varies in temperature between 1,652 °F (900 °C) and 2,192 °F (1,200 °C). The hotter the lava, the thinner and runnier it is, so the faster and farther it flows.

● Surtsey

The shield volcano Surtsey is located just off the southwest coast of Iceland, 11 miles (18 km) beyond Heimaey—another set of volcanic islands sitting on the Mid-Atlantic Ridge. Surtsey's eruption in 1963 built up this undersea volcano high enough from the ocean floor that it became one of the world's newest islands. Several eruptions happened one after the other, until 1967. Having been formed so recently, it is one of the most filmed and most thoroughly researched places on Earth.

▶ Fissure volcanoes do not have a traditional dome shape; instead, the lava erupts from huge cracks, or fissures, in the ground.

▶▶ Today, Surtsey has an area of 1.1 square miles (3 sq km). Its highest point stands 492 feet (150 m) above sea level. At first, the area was slightly larger, but the sea eroded some of the less consolidated lava. Despite the fact that Surtsey continued to erupt for three years after 1963, plants were spotted there as early as 1964, their seeds having been carried by the wind and water, and dropped by birds.

Types of volcanoes

Fissure volcanoes hardly look like volcanoes at all. Their lava is so hot, thin, and fluid that it flows great distances and never builds up a cone-shaped hill. In other volcanoes, lava comes out through the vent, but in fissure volcanoes, lava erupts through cracks in the ground—part of the plate boundary. The lava fills in any hollows, forming a smooth landscape.

Shield volcanoes are made of basic lava—hot, fast-flowing lava with a temperature around 2,192 °F (1,200 °C). These volcanoes form on constructive plate boundaries or over hot spots in the middle of a plate. Iceland's volcanoes, Surtsey and Hekla, are examples of constructive-margin volcanoes. Mauna Loa, Mauna Kea, and Kilauea on the Hawaiian islands are all hot spot features.

▲ Mount Pelée in the West Indies is an example of an acid dome volcano; the acidic lava that erupts from this volcano solidifies quickly, forming a steep-sided mountain.

Fissure volcano

▶ Base: Wide
▶ Sides: So gentle they can hardly be seen
▶ Example: Laki, Iceland

Shield volcano

▶ Base: Wide
▶ Sides: Gentle
▶ Examples: Mauna Loa, Hawaii; Surtsey, Iceland

Acid dome volcano

▶ Base: Narrow
▶ Sides: Steep
▶ Example: Mount Pelée, Martinique

Acidic lava is cooler than basic lava. It has a temperature of about 1,652 °F (900 °C). Solidifying quickly on contact with the air, this thick, sticky lava hardly flows any distance at all. Acid dome volcanoes, therefore, have a very distinctive shape, with narrow bases and steep sides. A spine forms at the top if lava solidifies so quickly that it never gets out of the vent. Mount Pelée on Martinique in the West Indies is a famous lava dome.

Ash and cinder cones grow more quickly than any other type of volcano. Ash and cinders are both very light materials containing lots of air, so the symmetrical sides of these volcanoes build up quickly. Because they are not strong, however, they easily weather away in the few years after each eruption. Paracutin in Mexico grew to more than 1,310 feet (400 m) in its first eruption, which began

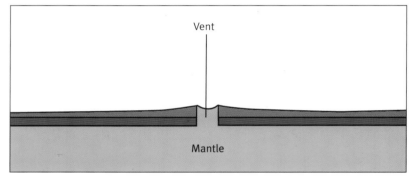

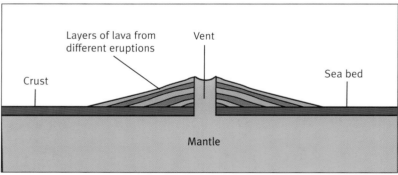

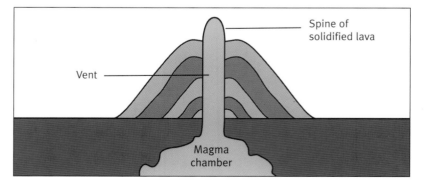

with no warning in the middle of a cornfield in 1943.

Composite volcanoes have alternate layers of acid lava and ash. As lava erupts at the surface, the release of pressure causes the gases to come out with an explosion. This explosion turns the lava to ash, which flies high into the air and then falls on the volcano's sides. Later, the lava begins to flow, spreading down the sides on top of the ash, making it stronger and less likely to erode over time.

The most explosive volcanoes are calderas. The buildup of gases in the magma chamber and vent is so great that a huge explosion follows, blowing away the whole summit of the volcano. A large depression, called a caldera, is left behind. A caldera may contain a lake or be flooded by the sea.

▲ Mount St. Helens in Washington is an example of a composite volcano. The volcano's lava is in the middle of the temperature range, so it flows for a moderate distance down the volcano sides before solidifying.

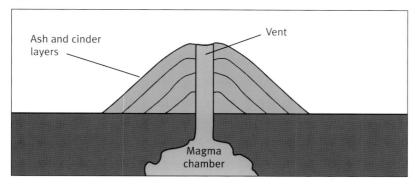

Ash and cinder volcano

▶ Base: Medium
▶ Sides: Moderately steep
▶ Example: Paracutin, Mexico

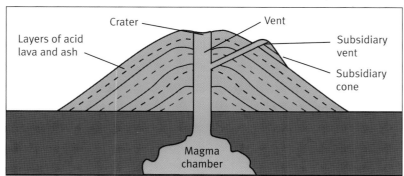

Composite volcano

▶ Base: Medium
▶ Sides: Moderately steep
▶ Example: Mount St. Helens

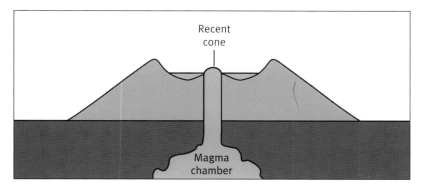

Caldera volcano

▶ Base: Medium
▶ Sides: Often cannot be distinguished
▶ Example: Krakatoa, Indonesia

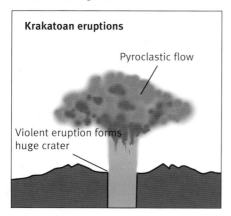

When Mount Vesuvius in Italy erupted in A.D. 79, it showered dust and ash over many miles. The entire city of Pompeii was buried in a matter of minutes, and the inhabitants were effectively mummified and preserved where they were killed.

Types of volcanic eruptions

The most important factor affecting the type of eruption of any volcano is whether its lava is basic or acidic. Basic lava (high temperature and very fluid) appears at constructive plate boundaries and at hot spots in the middle of a plate. Acidic lava (low temperature and thick) erupts at destructive margins. There are many types of volcanic eruptions; the five most varied examples are described below.

Icelandic and Hawaiian eruptions both involve basic lava. This means that the eruptions are relatively quiet, without explosions or great disruption to people. In an Icelandic eruption, lava flows gently from a fissure. Laki in Iceland is the best example, hence the name given to this type of eruption. Hawaiian eruptions are similar, except that the lava comes out of a vent at the center of the volcano, instead of from a long crack in the ground. All of Hawaii's volcanoes are over hot spots and are of this type.

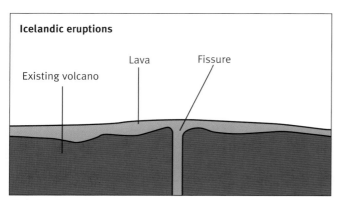

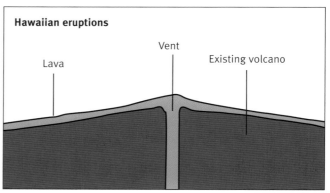

▲ Icelandic and Hawaiian eruptions involve basic (alkaline) lava. There are thin layers of lava, widely spread and moving gently, with little steam or other gases.

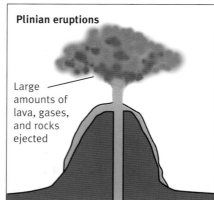

▲ Krakatoan, Peléan, and Plinian eruptions involve acidic lava. There is less lava, but more pyroclastic flow; they are very explosive.

▲ This illustration shows the nuée ardente—the massive cloud of hot gas and rocks—that destroyed St. Pierre, the capital of Martinique, during the eruption of Mount Pelée in 1902.

Krakatoan, Peléan, and Plinian eruptions all involve acidic lava. Krakatoan eruptions are exceptionally violent events. Much of the existing volcano can be exploded away each time the volcano erupts. They therefore never grow to be huge features in the landscape, but their wide, open shape is distinctive. Krakatoa in Indonesia, after which this type of eruption is named, and Crater Lake in the western United States, are both examples of volcanoes that erupt in this way.

Peléan eruptions are named after Mount Pelée in Martinique in the West Indies, which erupted in 1902. Although hardly any lava was involved in the eruption, the resulting pyroclastic flows and nuées ardentes caused severe damage. Super-hot, dense gases flowed downhill with terrific speed, carrying rocks and other debris along the way, burning everything in their path.

Plinian eruptions are unusual. Named after the Roman author Pliny the Younger, who recorded the eruption of Mount Vesuvius, which destroyed Pompeii in A.D. 79, they are probably the most violent volcanic eruptions. They produce large amounts of lava and pyroclastic materials. Dust, ash, and volcanic bombs are flung higher into the air than with any other eruption. For this reason, they are the most dangerous.

 Mount Pelée

Mount Pelée is part of the island arc that makes up the Lesser Antilles of the Caribbean. It has erupted 5 times in the last 500 years: in 1635, 1792, 1851–52, 1902–05, and 1929–32. The eruption of May 8, 1902, destroyed the capital city, St. Pierre, as the huge pyroclastic flow poured down the mountainside, destroying everything in its path. Nearly 30,000 people died—the largest number of casualties in a 20th-century eruption. Most of the destruction was caused by a nuée ardente—a hot, glowing cloud of gas carrying solid particles. The gases engulfed everything within a few feet of the ground.

Hot spots

Hot spots are areas on one of Earth's plates where hot rock bubbles up from the mantle. As the plate moves, the hot spot remains in the same place and keeps burning through the crust. This results in the formation of a chain of extinct volcanoes.

The impact of volcanoes

Volcanoes are found on every continent, and many countries are affected by volcanic eruptions. MEDCs are better able to deal with the aftermath of an eruption; they also have the technology available to monitor active volcanoes and to forecast possible eruptions. Also, in most of these countries, fewer people are forced to live on the sides of volcanoes in the risk zone, because population pressure is less severe. Three factors dictate the scale of the impact: the explosiveness of the eruption; how many people live in the danger area; and how developed the country is.

The Hawaiian volcanoes lie in the U.S., which is an MEDC. These shield volcanoes erupt gently, so they pose limited danger to life and property. Mauna Loa, Mauna Kea, and Kilauea are all peaks in this group of volcanic islands that lies over a hot spot in the Pacific Ocean.

Laki

Laki, in Iceland, is one of the best-known fissure volcanoes in the world. During the 1783 eruption, large amounts of sulfur gases were thrown out along with the lava. These gases are poisonous and very dangerous because they mix with oxygen and water vapor from the atmosphere to make—among other products—sulfuric acid. When the acidic vapor was washed out of the air by the rain, it killed many of the plants on the ground and poisoned the soil for several years. Crops would not grow, and livestock perished. During a 10-year period, 40,000 Icelanders died of starvation because their livelihoods had been destroyed.

▶ When fissure volcanoes like Laki in Iceland erupt, they eject rivers of thin, fast-flowing lava through cracks in the ground. They never build up into the cone shape normally associated with volcanoes.

The Nyiragongo volcano lies in the Democratic Republic of Congo (East Central Africa), part of a chain of volcanoes along the Great East African Rift Valley. It erupted on January 17, 2002, and severely affected the city of Goma. Even though the only material ejected was lava, which flowed relatively slowly (like Mauna Loa), the town was utterly devastated. Homes and other buildings were destroyed, roads were blocked, jobs were lost, and crops were destroyed. Half a million people were displaced. Because Congo is an LEDC, and because it is very remote and in a rain forest zone, help arrived very slowly. The situation was compounded when lava flowed over airport runways, preventing supplies from being flown in. Congo has few people trained to cope with emergencies and little equipment available. In many LEDCs, people are not insured against such disasters, so they have to start again from scratch. Nyiragongo continues to erupt very gently, which makes it difficult for people to restart their lives.

▲ Mauna Loa's summit is five miles (8 km) above its base on the Pacific Ocean floor. It makes up half the island of Hawaii and has been forming for almost one million years. It is one of the most active volcanoes on Earth, having erupted 35 times since the early 1800s. The last eruption was in 1984.

● The Pacific Ring of Fire

The Pacific Ring of Fire is so named because this ocean is ringed by numerous volcanoes. Almost all of the plate margins around the Pacific are destructive, so volcanoes are common. Only a few sections, such as the San Andreas Fault in California, consist of plate boundaries without volcanoes. There are even volcanoes located within the Pacific, such as those that form the Hawaiian islands; these are located over hot spots in Earth's crust. The Pacific is the most volcanically active region in the world, and some of the most famous volcanoes can be found in this region.

▶ Some of the best-known volcanoes in the world are part of the Pacific Ring of Fire. These include Mount Fuji in Japan, Mount Pinatubo in the Philippines, and Mount St. Helens in the U.S. The orange ring on the map marks the concentration of volcanoes around the plates.

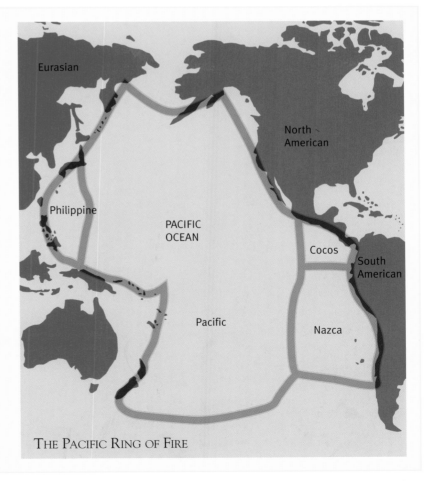

THE PACIFIC RING OF FIRE

Effects on the landscape

On May 18, 1980, an eruption blew the top off Mount St. Helens, a volcano in Washington. Before the eruption, the landscape of this area was considered so beautiful that it had been made a National Park. When the volcano erupted, this pristine, forested landscape was turned into a wasteland in a few short minutes.

During the early moments of the eruption, heat from the pyroclastic surge melted snow and ice on the mountaintop. Huge, destructive floods swept down the valleys, and the water mixed with soil, creating volcanic mudflows called lahars. Homes, roads, bridges, and trees were all washed away. The landscape was totally altered.

▼ The eruption of Mount St. Helens in 1980 was one of the worst volcanic eruptions of the 20th-century. Its effects were felt for hundreds of miles around the surrounding area.

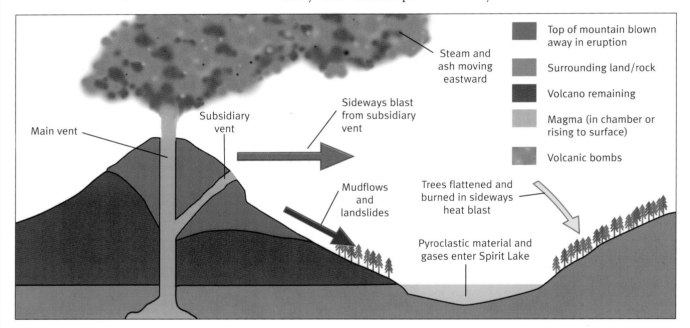

Steam and ash moving eastward

Sideways blast from subsidiary vent

Main vent

Subsidiary vent

Mudflows and landslides

Trees flattened and burned in sideways heat blast

Pyroclastic material and gases enter Spirit Lake

Top of mountain blown away in eruption

Surrounding land/rock

Volcano remaining

Magma (in chamber or rising to surface)

Volcanic bombs

On the volcano itself, the northern side of the mountain was shaken loose, causing a massive rock avalanche. The debris spread over 230 square miles (600 sq km). Almost 1,310 feet (400 m) were blown off the mountain's height. The cone shape of the top of the mountain was opened up into a wide crater.

The huge explosion from the subsidiary vent sent a shock wave of immensely hot gases sideways at 185 to 310 miles (300–500 km) per hour, flattening trees within the blast zone and incinerating the leaves, needles, and twigs of those farther away. Spirit Lake, which had been an important place for fishing and other recreation, was filled in with mud, rocks, and other debris. Lots of ash fell into the lake, and poisonous gases from the blast were dissolved in its water, making it very acidic. All its wildlife died.

A huge amount of ash was released by this Plinian eruption, turning the landscape a uniform shade of gray. The ash cloud spread eastward, ruining crops. Car engines were damaged, and visibility was so bad it was like being in a thick fog.

Scientists have been amazed at the speed with which plants and animals return after volcanic eruptions. Ash, when weathered, is quite fertile, and plants can take root in it. Eventually, even dense vegetation returns. Smaller, hardy plants capable of surviving in difficult conditions with poor soil begin the process by colonizing the area. Gradually, conditions improve—the soil becomes deeper and more fertile—and new plants start to grow as seeds are blown in from the surrounding area.

▼ An aerial view of the eruption of Mount St. Helens in 1980.

Positive aspects of volcanic eruptions

Much about volcanic eruptions is destructive and negative, but volcanoes can also bring huge benefits to people living near them. The two main ways are through agriculture and tourism. People can make their living out of both of these economic activities.

Some parts of the world have a severe shortage of agricultural land. Countries consisting of several small islands that have high populations—such as Indonesia—are always short of land for producing food. Volcanic lava undergoes weathering to form extremely rich soils. In a country where land is in short supply, such soils are very valuable.

Volcanic landscapes are incredibly beautiful, so people are prepared to travel to see them. Several have a thriving tourist industry. When Mount St. Helens showed signs of erupting in the spring of 1980, many people flocked to watch it happen, not realizing the dangers. Some were killed. Walkers, climbers, and water sports enthusiasts had regularly visited this scenic area before the eruption.

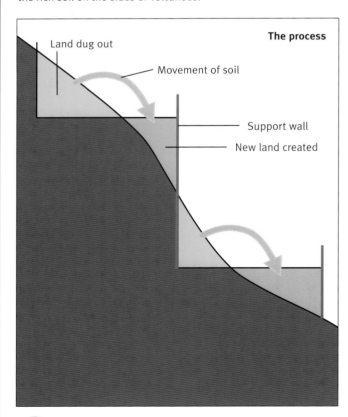

▲ Volcanoes can be huge tourist attractions, which can be important for the economy of a region. Here, tourists follow a trail to the volcanic peaks on Bartolome Island in Ecuador.

▼ To make the best use of the land available, people in countries such as Indonesia construct terraces in the rich soil on the sides of volcanoes.

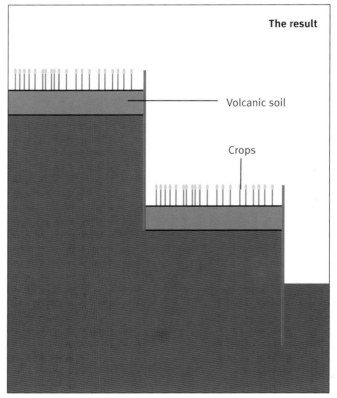

The process

Land dug out
Movement of soil
Support wall
New land created

The result

Volcanic soil
Crops

Geysers are a feature of some volcanic areas. Water is heated underground and explodes at the surface. Old Faithful is probably the best-known geyser in the world. Millions of people visit it every year. The special attraction of Old Faithful is that it spurts regularly, every 80 minutes, up to a height of 187 feet (57 m), lasting between 1 and 5 minutes each time.

Fumaroles are jets of steam that appear at the surface close to some volcanoes, where the crust can be as thin as 10 feet (3 m). Steam and sulfurous gases are emitted through cracks in the ground. Other hydrothermal phenomena are hot springs; some are found on New Zealand's South Island, along with hot mud pools that are said to have healing properties.

Some volcanic areas exploit cheap, natural energy. Iceland uses geothermal energy. Underground water is heated by magma, which provides all of Reykjavik, Iceland's capital, with cheap heating for homes and other buildings. Even tropical crops such as bananas can be grown in greenhouses heated by this volcanic resource.

▲ Geysers, such as Old Faithful in Yellowstone National Park, consist of deep wells in fissures in the rock. The water in the well is heated by the surrounding rocks until it suddenly boils and erupts.

◀ These greenhouses in Iceland are heated using geothermal energy, an environmentally friendly form of energy. It is readily available in Iceland because of the geological activity caused by the country's position on a plate boundary.

The Effects of
Earthquakes and Volcanoes

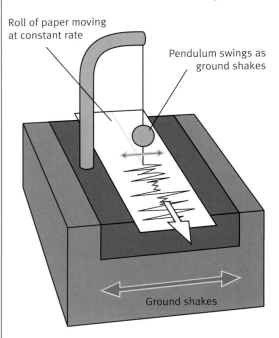

Roll of paper moving at constant rate

Pendulum swings as ground shakes

Ground shakes

▲ In a pendulum seismograph, the pendulum swings as the ground shakes. A roll of paper moves steadily (white arrow) beneath a pen, which records the earthquake waves. The broader the sweep, the more intense the earthquake.

▲ These seismographs are situated at the Parkfield laboratory in California, where seismologists predict and prepare for earthquakes that might hit the region.

In the parts of the world where volcanic eruptions and earthquakes take place, people live with the constant threat that their homes and land could be destroyed. In many countries, the occurrences of both earthquakes and volcanic eruptions can be predicted, and measures can be taken to prevent large-scale loss of life. Other countries, however, are not so well-equipped.

Seismology and the prediction of earthquakes

Seismology is the study and measurement of earthquakes. It is the main tool used for learning more about earthquakes in the hope of predicting when and where they may occur. Earthquakes are recorded using instruments called seismographs.

Even early seismographs were quite sensitive. The earliest known piece of equipment was invented by Choko, in China, in A.D. 136. His seismograph consisted of a copper vessel with eight dragon-head shapes attached to it, each with a ball in its mouth. Underneath each head was a metal frog with its mouth turned upward. During the shaking of an earthquake, some, or all, of the balls would drop from the dragons' into the frogs' mouths. The number of balls falling and the pattern of those that fell showed the strength and position of the earthquake. More recently, scientists have used a pendulum seismograph.

Modern seismology has provided much information about Earth's interior. Seismic tomography is an imaging method similar to that used in making CAT scans (X rays of the brain). The Parkfield research center in California is run by the U.S. Geological Survey (USGS) and is developing equipment that will pick up the slightest movements, from which scientists may be able to predict earthquakes in the future. The most up-to-date equipment is digital and uses broadband. It can sense even the slightest movement and works over a large range of frequencies. Rather than a pendulum moving, this equipment records the amount of energy needed to keep something still during the shaking.

Modern monitoring methods

Laser reflector: Detects small amounts of movement along a fault.
Ordinary surveying equipment: Used to determine whether the level of land has changed on either side of a fault.
Tiltmeter: Detects minor changes in the angle of the ground.
Gravity meter/magnetometer: Detects changes in the local magnetic field.
Radon gas counter: The amount of radon gas dissolved in underground water can increase before an earthquake.
Seismographs located underground: Used to pick up any foreshocks underground.
Strainmeter: Used to measure the stresses in the rocks.

▼ Strainmeters like this one are used to measure the movement of rock in faults like the San Andreas Fault in California.

The Morocco earthquake

An earthquake struck Morocco on February 25, 2004. The powerful earthquake measured 6.5 on the Richter scale and killed nearly 600 people. In the city of Al Hoceima, modern buildings had been constructed to withstand earthquakes. However, the poorer suburbs were severely affected as their lower-quality homes collapsed. Some of the worst-hit places were remote inland villages in the Rif mountains. Traditional mud huts in Tazaghin were completely flattened by the ground shaking.

▶ Rescuers use dogs to try to locate survivors buried under the rubble after the Moroccan earthquake in February 2004.

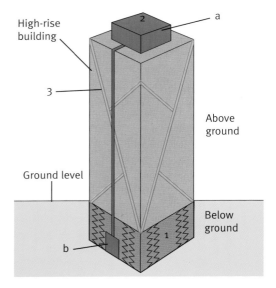

▼ Aseismic designs include: 1) rubber shock absorbers in the foundations to allow a building to shake safely; 2) concrete weights at the top of the building (a) that can be controlled by computers in the basement (b) and can be moved to balance the strain on the building; 3) cross-bracings to reduce damage to the building.

High-rise building

2

a

3

Above ground

Ground level

Below ground

b

1

Living with earthquakes

There are two main ways to make living in an earthquake zone safer: preventing damage by making buildings safer, and keeping people safe after an earthquake. Collapsing buildings are responsible for most deaths, but an aseismic design makes buildings less likely to fall. As a rule, taller buildings are more dangerous, but the proportions of the structure are also important. Buildings do not just shake during an earthquake—they can twist, too. Many countries now have strict building regulations, and newer buildings are much safer than older ones. Every earthquake gives engineers more information on which designs are the most effective.

No matter how clever the designs of earthquake-proof buildings become, there will always be a mess to clean up and rescue work to do following an earthquake, as well as simple survival in difficult conditions. The California state government encourages people to have the right

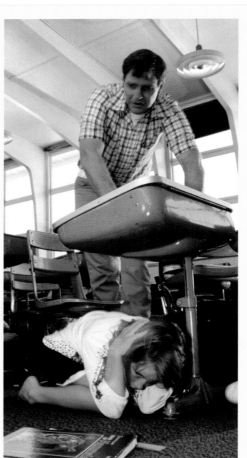

⬤ Emergency services

The work of emergency services after an earthquake needs very careful organization. The right people and equipment must be in the right place at the right time. This can be difficult when roads and telephone service are disrupted.

The Tokyo Gas Company overcomes this problem by using a radio network communication system. This can tell the central computer about pipeline damage. "Smart meters" automatically cut off gas in an earthquake measuring more than 5 on the Richter scale.

In California, computer systems are being developed to keep emergency services constantly up to date. The "Readicube" system will mean they know exactly where they are needed within five seconds of an earthquake.

Workplaces and schools already operate earthquake drills, so people know how to evacuate and are able to do a lot for themselves without emergency services.

◄ In areas like California, where earthquakes are a frequent occurrence, earthquake drills are conducted so everyone—even schoolchildren—knows what to do in an emergency.

equipment readily available in an emergency. This includes sturdy shoes and heavy gloves to help with rescue work, a garden hose to help with fire fighting, a change of clothing, a tent, candles, and matches.

Safe food and water supplies are perhaps the most important for survival, since disease can spread rapidly after an earthquake. One gallon (3.7 l) of water per person per day is required. Cooking may have to be outside, so camp stoves will be useful. Food needs to be dried, such as cereals and energy bars, or in cans, so it can be kept without refrigeration. A minimum of three days' worth of food is recommended. Large garbage bags to dispose of waste are needed, too.

Predicting a volcanic eruption—Mount Pinatubo

Mount Pinatubo lies on the island of Luzon, the most northerly of the larger islands of the Philippines. Situated on a destructive margin between the Philippine and Eurasian plates, this is one of the most active volcanic areas in the world. Pinatubo's most recent eruption, which began on June 15, 1991, was its first real activity for 400 years, but it proved to be the biggest eruption anywhere on Earth in the 20th century.

Due to the high volcanic risk in the Philippines, the country's volcanoes are constantly monitored by geologists and volcanologists who work together in the Philippine Institute of Volcanology and Seismology (PHIVOLCS), an organization funded by the government. They are helped by the USGS.

Before the eruption in 1991, several pieces of equipment were already in place on and around Mount Pinatubo. Tiltmeters were located on all of the Philippine volcanoes. These show any change in the angle of the ground and allow volcanologists to measure the development of the bulge on the side of the volcano prior to its eruption, which means they can evacuate the area in time. Seismographs were also used on Pinatubo. Volcanoes often shake as the pressure in the magma chamber below builds up and magma forces its way up the vent. Geologists monitoring Pinatubo noticed signs

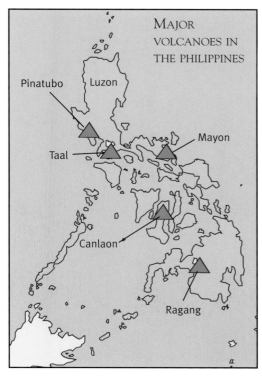

▲ The volcanoes in the Philippines have the potential to erupt with tremendous force. Even though Pinatubo had not been active for four centuries, other Filipino volcanoes, such as Mayon, farther southeast on Luzon, had been, so scientists already had some precautionary equipment in place.

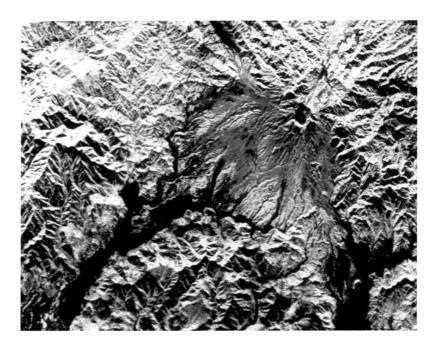

▶ This radar image of Mount Pinatubo shows how far the ash spread from the 1991 eruption (marked in red). The wide black channels leading from the volcano are mud deposits.

of such a build-up weeks before the actual eruption. Geologists use a standard hazard warning system to assess whether and when evacuation is necessary:

Level 1: Steam comes out of the ground; tiny earthquakes are picked up on the monitoring equipment.
Level 2: Continuous steam and gas emissions; some regular earthquake activity.
Level 3: Greatly increased earthquake activity; volcanic shaking starts.
Level 4: Dome of viscous magma appears; more earthquakes and tremors; ash emissions.
Level 5: First large explosive eruption; ash output increases quickly.

It is often difficult to decide when, if at all, people should be evacuated from an area. If the "safe" decision is made and people are evacuated but no event occurs, unnecessary disruption has been caused, and there is the risk that in the future the geologists will not be believed. If the decision to evacuate is made too late and the volcano erupts, severe damage to property and loss of life may occur. In the case of Pinatubo, the scientists made the right decision and ordered an evacuation. Local people picked up their belongings and walked away. Although there were still deaths, many of those were caused by lahars triggered by the torrential rains that came with the monsoon. The situation could have been much worse.

▼ Geologists carefully monitor volcanic activity, including gas emissions, in order to determine whether or not to evacuate an area.

Pinatubo statistics

- 176 billion cubic feet (5 billion cu m) of ash and other pyroclastic materials ejected
- Eruption column 11 miles (18 km) wide and 19 miles (30 km) high
- Dust and ash in the air spread around the world in the upper atmosphere
- Global temperatures initially dropped by 5.4 °F (3 °C)
- Global temperatures lower by 1.8 °F (1 °C) on average for three years
- 740 dead
- 184 injured
- 23 missing, bodies never found
- More than one million homeless

▼ More than 176 billion cubic feet (5 billion cu m) of ash and other material were ejected when Pinatubo erupted in 1991. More than 490 feet (150 m) of the volcano was blasted away during the eruption.

Armero

In 1985, the town of Armero in Colombia (an LEDC) experienced a huge volcanic disaster. Lying on a subduction zone between the Nazca and South American plates, the eruption of the Nevado del Ruiz volcano was moderately explosive, but few people lived close enough to be directly affected. However, snow and ice lying over the mountain melted. Water mixed with soil and debris to create a huge mudslide, which destroyed everything in its path. Armero, lying down-valley from the volcano, suffered its full force. It happened during the night, so people were unable to see the hazard approaching. Armero's survivors eventually moved on, unable to live with the physical and emotional destruction the volcano had caused.

▶ The town of Armero in Colombia was destroyed by the mudflows that resulted from the eruption of the Nevado del Ruiz volcano—23,000 people died in the disaster.

MAJOR VOLCANOES IN ITALY

Campi Flegri

Vesuvius

Strombi

Vulcano

Etna

Living with volcanoes—Mount Etna

Mount Etna is Europe's highest (10,500 feet, or 3,200 m) and most active volcano. Its eruptions have been documented since 1500 B.C. Etna has erupted 200 times since then, often close to settlements. Volcanic soil makes this area one of the most fertile in the entire Mediterranean; however, Etna's frequent eruptions threaten cultivated areas, homes, and even whole settlements. As more people are able to travel, the local tourist industry has grown rapidly in recent years, which brings a great deal of money into the area. Tourists come to see the spectacular landscape, hot lava, the bubbling activity within the crater, and the colorful pyroclastic displays. The volcano gives many opportunities to view nature's fireworks.

In fact, the chance of Etna's lava engulfing a nearby house

is very small. Etna's acidic lava flows so slowly that it is possible to get out of its way. The main impact is from small falls of ash or grit-sized fragments. Sometimes, individual buildings are damaged or destroyed. In the past, however, Etna has experienced cataclysmic eruptions. Major eruptions happened in the years 1169 and 1669, exactly 500 years apart. If the same time gap continues between eruptions, the next one would be due in 2169.

In many cases, the advantages of living in these fertile regions outweighs the risks. As understanding of volcanoes and seismic activity grows, people can lead their lives more confidently in the shadows of volcanoes.

▼ A volcanologist wearing a heatproof suit on the solidified lava around Mount Etna in Italy. In 2001, Etna began to pour out its lava flows once again, with 16 separate eruptions. Five vents produced thick lava with lots of steam and smoke. The town of Nicolosi was especially threatened, and lava movement was monitored closely.

Glossary

acid dome volcano A volcano with a steep-sided body; solidified lava blocks the vent of the volcano, making the top section higher and possibly wider.

acid lava Thick, sticky, slow-flowing lava with a temperature between 1,652 °F (900 °C) and 2,192 °F (1,200 °C).

aseismic Any engineering method that makes a building more resistant to earthquake damage.

ash and cinder cone A volcano with explosive eruptions of ash but little or no lava; easily eroded because its material is not very resistant.

basalt A dark-colored igneous rock, often found in oceanic plates or in the material welling up at constructive plate margins.

basic lava Thin, fast-flowing lava with a temperature higher than 2,192 °F (1,200 °C).

caldera A large volcanic crater formed by the collapse of a volcano's cone during a very explosive eruption.

collision zone A plate boundary where two continental plates move toward each other.

composite volcano A volcano made of alternate layers of ash and lava; it may have side (subsidiary) vents and cones.

cone One of the simplest volcano formations, built by fragments (ejecta) ejected from a volcanic vent, piling up around the vent in the shape of a cone with a central crater.

conservative boundary A boundary where two plates slide past each other, sometimes getting stuck and causing earthquakes when they jolt free.

constructive boundary A boundary where two plates move apart and new crust is created.

continental crust Parts of Earth's crust composed of light rocks. They are made of compounds containing lots of silica (sand) and aluminium.

continental drift The theory by Alfred Wegener explaining why Earth's continents appear to move and split into different sections.

convection current A current of hot magma in the mantle. It rises from the lower part of the mantle, where temperatures are hottest, toward the crust.

core The central part of Earth, made of iron and nickel.

crater The top section of the vent of a volcano, usually blocked by solidified lava between eruptions.

crust The outermost layer of Earth.

destructive boundary A boundary at which two plates move toward each other. The denser plate dips down below the other and melts.

earthquake lights Unexplained flashes of light that appear just before or during an earthquake, usually lasting a few seconds each time.

epicenter The point on Earth's surface vertically above the focus, where the worst damage usually occurs during an earthquake.

fault A fracture in Earth's crust that displaces the rocks on either side of it.

fissure A huge crack in the ground, often part of a plate boundary.

fissure volcano A volcano in which lava erupts along the fissure and is able to flow far from the vent.

focus The point underground from which an earthquake originates.

fold mountains Mountains made of a set of parallel ridges caused when the continental rocks "pile up" at a destructive boundary or collision zone.

fumarole A vent from which volcanic vapors escape; from the Latin *fumariolum*, a smoke-hole.

geothermal Energy that may be generated by the utilization of naturally occurring geological heat sources. It is a form of renewable energy.

geyser A natural underground stream that throws out hot water and jets of steam from the ground.

hot spot An area on Earth's surface where the crust is quite thin. Magma can break through and form a volcano.

hydrodynamic effect The smashing of structures such as roads or bridges by a tsunami.

hydrostatic event When buildings and other structures are forced inland or pulled back into the sea by a tsunami.

hydrothermal Relating to water heated underground by volcanic activity.

intraplate A point within a plate not near its edges.

island arc A chain of islands formed when volcanoes created on the ocean floor grow tall enough to break the surface.

L waves Longitudinal waves; earthquake waves that begin as P or S waves but then move along Earth's surface.

lahar A kind of mudslide made of volcanic materials and water.

lava Magma when it has broken through Earth's surface.

LEDC Less Economically Developed Country; these countries usually have poorer communication and emergency services and suffer more severely from the effects of earthquakes and volcanoes.

magma Molten rock in Earth's mantle.

magma chamber The space beneath a volcano in which the magma is held before an eruption.

mantle The layer of Earth above the core and beneath the crust.

MEDC More Economically Developed Country; these countries are usually better prepared for the consequences of earthquakes and volcanoes.

Mercalli scale A scale to measure the damage done by earthquakes. It is not connected to the energy of the earthquake. If there is more settlement in an area, there is likely to be more damage, so the level is higher.

Mid-Atlantic Ridge The name given to the mid-ocean ridge stretching down the center of the Atlantic Ocean.

mudflow Mud and sediment saturated with water and moving rapidly downhill or in a channel. Also called a lahar.

nuée ardente A cloud of extremely hot gas that "rolls" down the side of an erupting volcano.

oceanic crust Parts of Earth's crust made of denser rocks.

P waves Primary or "push" waves; earthquake waves that travel from the epicenter up to the surface of Earth.

plate A section of Earth's crust.

plate tectonics The theory developed in the 1960s from earlier ideas of continental drift. It explains the nature of Earth's plates, the way they move, and the features that form at their boundaries, including earthquakes and volcanoes.

pyroclastic flow Volcanic ash, dust, bombs, and other fragments in hot, dense gases, which travel downhill at high speeds.

Richter scale A scale for measuring the energy or magnitude of an earthquake.

S waves Secondary or "shake" waves; earthquake waves that travel away from an epicenter.

seismic waves Movements in Earth's crust that indicate that an earthquake may be about to happen or is already happening.

seismogram The printout from a seismograph.

seismograph Equipment used to measure the amount of ground shaking associated with an earthquake or volcano.

seismologist A scientist or geologist who studies earthquakes.

shield volcano A wide-based volcano with basic, fast-flowing lava.

shock effects When debris carried by a tsunami damages buildings and kills or injures people.

subduction zone A destructive plate boundary where a dense oceanic plate is forced down below a lighter continental one, where it melts.

tsunami A large wave caused by an undersea earthquake or volcanic eruption.

USGS United States Geological Survey—the main group of scientists working on volcanoes and earthquakes and their prediction throughout the world.

vent The hollow central part of a volcano, out of which lava, steam, and other materials are ejected.

volcanologist A scientist or geologist who studies volcanoes and their behavior.

weathering The wearing away of rock by rain, frost, plant roots, and animals burrowing.

Further Information

Books

Engelbert, Phillis. *Dangerous Planet: The Science of Natural Disasters*. Detroit: UXL, 2001.

Gifford, Clive. *The Kingfisher Geography Encyclopedia*. Boston: Kingfisher, 2003.

Knight, Linsay, and Elridge M. Moores, ed. *Volcanoes & Earthquakes*. New York: Barnes & Noble Books, 2003.

Oxlade, Chris. *Earth's Changing Landscapes: Earthquakes & Volcanoes*. North Mankato, Minn.: Smart Apple Media, 2005.

Ritchie, David, and Alexander E. Gates. *Encyclopedia of Earthquakes and Volcanoes*. New York: Checkmark Books / Facts on File, 2001.

Web sites

http://www.seismo.unr.edu/htdocs/abouteq.html
Sponsored by the Nevada Seismological Laboratory, this site addresses frequently asked questions about earthquakes and provides information from the Nevada Earthquake Safety Council.

http://www.pbs.org/wnet/savageearth/
Learn about Earth's major tectonic plates and the natural hazards caused by their movement, such as earthquakes and volcanoes.

http://volcano.und.nodak.edu/volcanoes.html
A Web site dedicated to volcanoes, including information on current eruptions, movie clips of volcanic activity, and information on volcanoes of other planets and moons.

http://www.usgs.gov/
Home page of the U.S. Geological Survey, with resources and news stories about the geography and geology of the United States, including information and updates about earthquakes and volcanoes.

http://www.volcanolive.com/
A site packed with links to information on all aspects of volcanoes and volcanic activity, including maps of the world's volcanoes and how to deal with volcanic disasters.

Index

Acknowledgements

Picture Credits

Cover: (t) Krafft/ Explorer/Science Photo Library (bl) Peter Menzel/Science Photo Library (br) Professor Stewart Lowther/ Science Photo Library 6 Krafft/Explorer/Science Photo Library 7(t) Peter Menzel/Science Photo Library 7(b) Adam G. Sylvester/ Science Photo Library 9(b) Krafft/Hoa-Qui/Science Photo Library 11(t) © Galen Rowell/Corbis 12(l) James King-Holmes/Science Photo Library 13(t) Peter Menzel/Science Photo Library 14(t) © Wolfgang Rattay/Reuters/Corbis 14(b) © Bettmann/ Corbis 15(t) Joe Pasieka/Science Photo Library 15(b) NASA/ Science Photo Library 16 © PBNJ Productions/ Corbis 17 Jean-Loup Charmet/Science Photo Library 18 © Reuters/Corbis 19(t) © Bettmann/Corbis 19(b) Lynette Cook/Science Photo Library 20(b) © Lloyd Cluff/Corbis 21 © Romeo Ranoco/ Reuters/Corbis 22 Courtesy of Digital Globe 23 © Pierre Vauthey/Corbis Sygma 24(t) © James L. Amos/ Corbis 25(t) Professor Stewart Lowther/Science Photo Library 26(t) © Bettmann/Corbis 27(t) David Hardy/Science Photo Library 28 David Hardy/Science Photo Library 29(t) NASA/ Science Photo Library 31 NASA/Science Photo Library 32(t) © Kevin Schafer/Corbis 33(t) David Halpern/Science Photo Library 33(b) Martin Bond/Science Photo Library 34(b) Peter Menzel/ Science Photo Library 35(t) David Parker/Science Photo Library 35(b) © Andrea Comas/Reuters/ Corbis 36(b) David Parker/ Science Photo Library 38(t) NASA/Science Photo Library 38(b) British Antarctic Survey/Science Photo Library 39 © Alberto Garcia/Corbis 40(t) © Jacques Languevin/Corbis 41 Jeremy Bishop/Science Photo Library